D1103979

Makers as
INNOVATORS
JUNIOR

# Using Light to Make Shadow Puppets

**By Kristin Fontichiaro**

Published in the United States of America by
**Cherry Lake Publishing**
Ann Arbor, Michigan
www.cherrylakepublishing.com

Series Editor: Kristin Fontichiaro
Reading Adviser: Marla Conn, MD, Ed., Literacy Specialist,
Read-Ability, Inc.
Photo Credits: Cover and pages 4 and 6; Pixabay/CC0 Creative
Commons; page 8, Maasaak/Wikimedia / CC BY-SA 4.0 /
tinyurl.com/y89honxu; pages 10, 14, 16, 18, and 20; Kristin
Fontichiaro; page 12, liz west/flickr / CC BY 2.0 / tinyurl.com/
yclytj5o

Copyright © 2018 by Cherry Lake Publishing
All rights reserved. No part of this book may be reproduced or
utilized in any form or by any means without written permission
from the publisher.

Library of Congress Cataloging-in-Publication Data has been filed and is available
at catalog.loc.gov

Cherry Lake Publishing would like to acknowledge the work of the Partnership for
21st Century Learning. Please visit *www.p21.org* for more information.

Printed in the United States of America
Corporate Graphics

A Note to Adults: Please review the instructions for the activities in this book before allowing children to do them. Be sure to help them with any activities you do not think they can safely complete on their own.

A Note to Kids: Be sure to ask an adult for help with these activities when you need it. Always put your safety first!

# Table of Contents

Shadows................................................ 5

Shadow Puppets in the Past.................... 7

Setting Up a Screen.............................. 9

In the Spotlight.................................... 11

Selecting a Story................................. 13

Let's Make Puppets!.............................. 15

Playing with Shadows............................ 17

Practice, Practice, Practice.................... 19

Showtime!........................................... 21

Glossary............................................. 22

Find Out More...................................... 23

Index................................................. 24

About the Author................................. 24

The sunlight is coming from the left side of the photo. The dog blocks the light, making the shadow appear on the right.

# Shadows

Have you ever noticed a gray outline of yourself on the sidewalk? Was the sun out that day? That's your shadow! When you stand between the sun and the sidewalk, you block the sunlight. That's why part of the sidewalk looks dark. On a cloudy day, we see fewer sidewalk shadows. You need bright light to make a shadow.

Indonesian shadow puppets tell stories from the past.

# Shadow Puppets in the Past

Light and shadows have interested people for hundreds of years. In Indonesia, people stayed up until it got dark. They sat on one side of a white sheet or screen for hours. A puppeteer and **musicians** sat on the other side with some lamps. When the puppeteer put puppets against the sheet, they made shadows. Today, we don't have to stay up late to use shadow puppets. We can use electricity instead!

Ask some adults if they have ever made shadow puppets with their hands. What shapes can you make with yours?

# Setting Up a Screen

The screen is where your shadows will appear. For this book, we will use a wall as our screen. Find a room that has walls with a light color. You will need an **outlet** nearby so you can plug in a lamp. You might need an adult to help you move furniture.

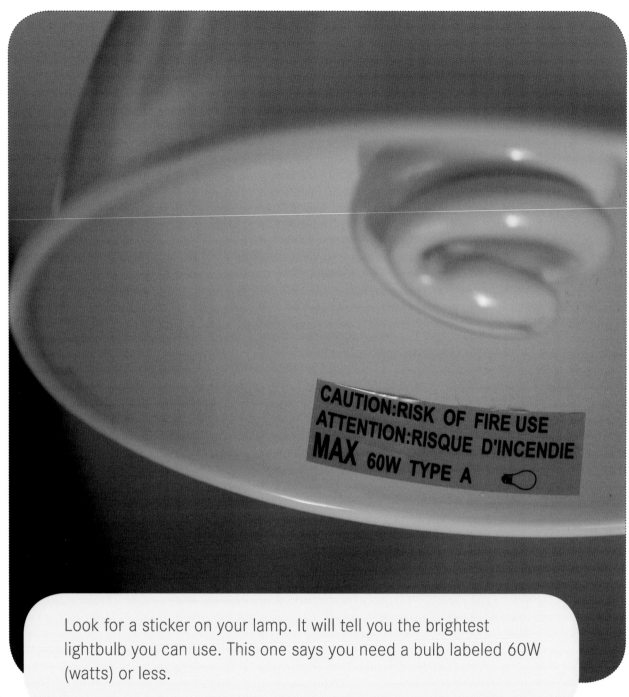

CAUTION:RISK OF FIRE USE
ATTENTION:RISQUE D'INCENDIE
MAX 60W TYPE A

Look for a sticker on your lamp. It will tell you the brightest lightbulb you can use. This one says you need a bulb labeled 60W (watts) or less.

# In the Spotlight

Ask an adult to help you find a lamp with a bright bulb in it. Check the lamp so you know the highest **wattage** the bulb can be. Put the lamp on a sturdy table. Turn it on and point it safely toward the wall. Do you like the size of the light it makes? Move the table closer or farther from the wall. This will control the size of the light.

## Safety First!

Lightbulbs are made of glass. They can get hot and break. Set up your lamp in a safe place. Make sure no one can knock it over. Stack books on all sides of the lamp so it can't move. Cover the cord with chairs so no one can trip.

*Aesop's Fables* is a collection of short stories that teach a lesson. "The Lion and the Mouse" is a famous example.

# Selecting a Story

Every puppet show needs a story. You can make one up. Or choose a picture book to read out loud. You can also find good story ideas in *Aesop's Fables*. Choose a story with just a few characters when you are a beginning puppeteer. You can only have one puppet in each hand!

## Casting Call

Most shadow plays have a **narrator**. Other people move the puppets or play music. Do you want your show to be bigger? Ask more friends to help!

It doesn't matter if you draw lines or tape pieces on your puppet. Those things won't show up on the shadow!

# Let's Make Puppets!

Get some cardstock or thick paper. Cardstock won't flop over, but it is still easy to cut. Any color is okay to get. People will see the shadow, not the color. Think about the shape you want to see on the screen. Draw it. Cut it out with scissors. Turn on the lamp. Hold your puppet up to the wall. Do you like the shadow it makes? If not, change it! Tape your finished puppet to a pencil, chopstick, or other long stick.

Playing can give you new ideas. When we played, our bird puppet looked silly on a stick. So we hung it from a ribbon instead!

# Playing with Shadows

It's good to play with puppets and shadows before you present your show. This will teach you how shadows work. Here are some things to try.

1.  Hold your puppet straight up in front of the wall. What happens if you turn it sideways?

2.  How will your puppet enter the show? Does it pop up? Fly in? Walk in from the side?

3.  How can your puppet show that it is happy, sad, or curious?

Hold your puppets really close to the wall. See what happens? The shadows are the same size as your puppet. What happens if you move the puppets closer to the lamp? Try it and see!

# Practice, Practice, Practice

Turn on the lamp. Ask the narrator to read the story out loud. Practice having your puppets enter and exit. If you have many puppeteers, practice staying out of each other's way! Try adding music or **sound effects**. Ask an adult if you can use a pot as a drum. Shake beans in a container. Rub a wooden spoon on a grater. Keep practicing until everybody feels comfortable.

Making tickets can add fun to your show. Use words like "Admit One" on your ticket. That means "Let one person see the show."

# Showtime!

Now you are ready to put on a show. Make posters to **advertise** your show. Invite your friends or family to be the **audience**.

When they arrive, collect their tickets and give them a **program**. Ask them to sit behind the puppeteers. Have the narrator face the audience. Turn on the lamp and start the show!

## Break a Leg!

It's bad luck to say "good luck" to a performer. Say "break a leg" instead. You don't really want them to get hurt. You are saying something bad so that something good will happen instead!

# Glossary

**advertise** (AD-vur-tize) to give information about something that you want people to know about

**audience** (AWD-ee-uhns) people who come to watch a show

**musicians** (myoo-ZIH-shuhns) people who play music

**narrator** (NAYR-ay-tur) a person who tells a story

**outlet** (OUT-let) a place where electric-powered things can be plugged in and connected to electricity

**program** (PROH-gram) a booklet that gives you information about a show you're about to see

**sound effects** (SOWND eh-FEKTS) noises in a show, such as a drum that sounds like someone walking

**wattage** (WAT-ij) the amount of electricity you can get from a lightbulb

# Find Out More

## Books

Jacobs, Frank. *Fun with Hand Shadows.* Mineola, NY: Dover Publications, 1996.

Rau, Dana Meachen. *Super Cool Science Experiments: Light.* Ann Arbor, MI: Cherry Lake Publishing, 2010.

## Web Sites

### Kidspot—Make a Shadow Puppet Theatre

*www.kidspot.com.au/things-to-do/activities/make-a-shadow-puppet-theatre*

Learn how to make a shadow puppet screen out of a cardboard box.

### PBS Kids—ZOOM Playhouse

*http://pbskids.org/zoom/activities/playhouse*

Find plays that you can use for your puppet shows.

# Index

adults, 9, 11, 19
advertising, 21
*Aesop's Fables,* 13
audiences, 21

cardstock, 15
characters, 13

furniture, 9

history, 7

Indonesia, 7

lamps, 7, 9, 11
luck, 21

music, 7, 13, 19

narrators, 13, 19, 21

outlets, 9

posters, 21
practice, 17, 19
puppets, 7, 13, 15, 17, 19

safety, 11
screens, 7, 9, 15
shadows, 5, 17
sound effects, 19
stories, 13, 19

wattage, 11

## About the Author

Kristin Fontichiaro teaches at the University of Michigan School of Information. Her office is full of supplies for making things.